GEOGRAPHY FACT FILES

RIVERS

Mandy Ross

A⁺
Smart Apple Media

GEOGRAPHY FACT FILES

COASTLINES

DESERTS

MOUNTAINS

OCEANS

POLAR REGIONS

RIVERS

First published in 2004 by Hodder Wayland

338 Euston Road, London NW1 3BH, United Kingdom

Hodder Wayland is an imprint of Hodder Children's Books, a division of Hodder Headline Limited. This edition published under license from Hodder Children's Books. All rights reserved.

Produced for Hodder Wayland by

Monkey Puzzle Media Ltd

Gissing's Farm, Fressingfield, Suffolk IP21 5SH

United Kingdom

Copyright © 2004 Hodder Wayland

Editor	Catherine Burch
Designer	Jamie Asher
Picture Researcher	Lynda Lines and Frances Bailey
Illustrator	Michael Posen
Consultant	Michael Allaby

Published in the United States by Smart Apple Media

2140 Howard Drive West

North Mankato, Minnesota 56003

U.S. publication copyright © 2005 Smart Apple Media International copyright reserved in all countries. No part of this book may be reproduced in any form without written permission from the publisher.

Printed in China

Library of Congress Cataloging-in-Publication Data

Ross, Mandy.

Rivers / by Mandy Ross.

p. cm. — (Geography fact files)

Includes bibliographical references.

ISBN 1-58340-429-5

1. Rivers—Juvenile literature. 2. Stream ecology—Juvenile literature. [1. Rivers. 2. Stream ecology. 3. Ecology.] I. Title. II. Series.

GB1203.8.R67 2004

551.48'3—dc22   2003070387

9 8 7 6 5 4 3 2 1

Acknowledgements

We are grateful to the following for permission to reproduce photographs: Aerofilms.com 17 bottom; Associated Press 11 bottom (Apichart Weera Wong); Corbis back cover bottom (Ales Fevzer), 13 bottom (Hulton-Deutsch), 27 (Kevin Fleming), 42 (Ales Fevzer); Digital Vision 47; Ecoscene 41 (Stephen Coyne); FLPA 6 (Minden Pictures), 29 bottom (David Hosking), 37 top (Skylight); Getty Images front cover (Jeremy Woodhouse); Nature Picture Library 10 (Pete Oxford), 19 (Paul N Johnson), 21 top (A and S Chandola), 23 top (Vincent Munier), 24 (John Cancalosi), 28 (Staffan Widstrand), 40 top (Jean Roche); NHPA 4 (David Woodfall), 18 (NASA/T&T Stack), 20 (David Woodfall), 40 bottom (David Woodfall); Edward Parker 25; Popperfoto 38, 39 (Juda Ngwenya/Reuters); Robert Harding Picture Library 3 middle (T Waltham), 3 bottom (Paul Allen), 5 bottom (Roy Rainford), 9, 11 top, 14, 15 (T Waltham), 22 (Paul Allen), 23 bottom (Gary Schultz), 29 top (Gavin Hellier); Science Photo Library 36 (Martin Bond); Still Pictures 1 (S J Krasemann), 3 top (BAV/Helga Lade GmbH), 5 top (BAV/Helga Lade GmbH), 17 top (S J Krasemann), 26 (Hartmut Schwarzbach), 33 bottom (Jorgen Schytte), 35 (Jim Wark), 37 bottom (Michael Coupard), 43 (J Sackermann/Das Fotoarchiv), 44 (Uniphoto International); Topham Picturepoint 13 top (Rob Crandall/Image Works), 21 bottom (Tom Brakefield/ Image Works), 30 (Jim Pickerell/Image Works), 31 (Lee Snider/Image Works), 32 (Owen Humphreys/PA), 46 (Lee Snider/Image Works); WaterAid 45 (Jon Spaull).

Title page picture: A meandering river in Alaska.

CONTENTS

WHAT IS A RIVER?

A river is a large stream of fresh flowing water. High in the mountains, small streams gather together to form a river rushing down through hills and valleys. Lower down most rivers flow more slowly through flatter land until they reach the sea. River environments are very important because all life needs water to survive.

Most streams begin high in the mountains, like this one in Snowdonia, Wales.

There are rivers all around the world. Rivers flow through icy landscapes, freezing over during the coldest seasons. They flow through tropical rain-forests and through deserts. Many cities are built on the banks of great rivers, growing out of villages inhabited since ancient times.

Rivers are a source of life for humans, animals, and plants. They offer fish to eat and water to drink. They irrigate crops, provide transportation routes, and serve as popular places for recreation. The power of flowing water can be harnessed to create **renewable energy**. However, water can also be dangerous. When rivers flood, or when the water is polluted, rivers can threaten the very life they sustain.

FACT FILE

RIVER FACTS
• The world's longest river is the Nile River, in Africa. It is about 4,123 miles (6,650 km) long.
• The Roe River, in Montana, is one of the world's shortest rivers. It is just 200 feet (61 m) long—about as long as 15 cars!
• Rivers make up only a tiny fraction of the world's fresh water—just 0.003 percent. Lakes and inland seas make up 0.6 percent, and the rest is in ice caps, **glaciers**, **groundwater**, and in the soil.

THE MISSISSIPPI RIVER

The name "Mississippi" comes from Algonkian, a Native American language, from the words misi, meaning "big," and sipi, meaning "water." The Mississippi River (left) starts as a clear, winding stream. Many rivers join it along its 3,702-mile (5,971 km) course, including the Missouri, Ohio, and Red Rock. Downriver, it stretches more than 1.2 miles (2 km) wide in places. The Mississippi loops and curves along its path, but it has been straightened in places to allow ships to pass more safely. It is one of the busiest shipping waterways in the world.

The Mississippi passes through 10 U.S. states and is the longest river in North America.

Many great cities have grown up at a crossing point over a river, like the river Seine in Paris, France.

River water is a shared and precious resource. What is done to a river in one place may affect it a long way downstream, so rivers must be treated carefully to protect people's needs and the needs of the wildlife that depends on them.

RIVERS AND THE WATER CYCLE

Rivers are part of a never-ending **water cycle**. Most rivers start high in the mountains where plenty of rain and snow fall. Rainwater and melted snow flow down the mountains and hills, and eventually out into the salty ocean. There the sun and wind cause some of the water to evaporate, then **condense** into tiny droplets, forming clouds, and later fall as rain.

GREAT RIVERS

Some of the great rivers of the world flow thousands of miles, traveling across whole continents. Some are so wide that it is impossible to see one bank from another. These great rivers are best viewed from the air or even from space. Which is the world's greatest river? It depends upon what's being measured.

There are many different ways to measure the size of a river. One way is to measure its length, from its beginning, or **source**, to the place where it meets the sea, called the mouth. Rivers do not flow in straight lines—they bend and curve—so the measurement has to follow all the curves.

Another way of comparing the size of rivers is to measure the amount of water flowing in them, called the **discharge**. The discharge changes during the year, so an average figure is usually given.

For most of its length, the Amazon River is between four and six miles (6–10 km) wide.

FACT FILE

THE WORLD'S LONGEST RIVERS

RIVER	OUTFLOW	LENGTH including main tributaries
Nile	Mediterranean Sea	4,123 miles (6,650 km)
Amazon-Ucayali-Apurimac	South Atlantic Ocean	3,968 miles (6,400 km)
Yangtze	East China Sea	3,906 miles (6,300 km)
Mississippi-Missouri-Red Rock	Gulf of Mexico	3,702 miles (5,971 km)
Yenisey-Baikal-Selenga	Kara Sea	3,435 miles (5,540 km)
Yellow River	East China Sea	3,388 miles (5,464 km)
Ob-Irtysh	Gulf of Ob	3,354 miles (5,410 km)
Parana	South Atlantic Ocean	3,026 miles (4,880 km)
Congo	Atlantic Ocean	2,914 miles (4,700 km)
Amur-Argun	Sea of Okhotsk	2,755 miles (4,444 km)

RIVERS WITH THE LARGEST DRAINAGE AREA

RIVER	AREA (000 sq mi)	AREA (000 sq km)
Amazon	2,800	7,180
Congo	1,491	3,822
Mississippi-Missouri	1,256	3,221
Ob	1,160	2,975
Nile	1,124	2,881

A map showing the world's greatest rivers.

A third way of comparing rivers is to measure the area of land that drains into the river. This measurement includes all the land that is drained by streams and small rivers or **tributaries** that flow into the main river. This total area is called a river's **drainage area**, or basin.

The Amazon is only the second-longest river in the world, but it has by far the biggest discharge. This is because the Amazon has the biggest drainage area, including about 40 percent of the continent of South America. Most of the rivers of the northern half of South America flow into the Amazon, because mountains and high land cut off other routes to the sea. Much of the continent's water flows east into the Amazon, creating a giant river. About one-fifth of all the world's river water flows out of the Amazon into the Atlantic Ocean.

SPRINGS AND SOURCES

Where do rivers start? Most begin on high ground or in the mountains. Many of the world's greatest rivers start as springs and tiny streams in high mountains. For instance, the source of the Ganges River, in Asia, is high in the Himalayan mountains. Searching for the source of the river is a challenge that has inspired many explorers.

High in the mountains there is heavy rain and snowfall. The rain that falls on the mountainsides runs quickly down the steep slopes into little channels called rills. These rills join together to form small streams, and as the streams run down the mountain they also join together, gradually forming a wide river.

Streams and rivers are also fed by melt-water, which flows down the mountainsides when warmer weather causes snow and ice high in the mountains to melt. If the weather warms up quickly, melting a lot of snow, rivers can suddenly get much deeper, and sometimes flood.

PEOPLE FILE

WHO FOUND THE NILE SOURCE?

More than 2,000 years ago, the Greek historian Herodotus wrote: "Of the source of the Nile no one can give any account." In fact, the Nile River has two sources, the Blue Nile and the White Nile. The first European to see the source of the Blue Nile was Father Pedro Páez, a Spanish Jesuit, in 1618. In 1937, a German explorer, Dr. Burkhart Waldecker, traced the source of the White Nile back to its southernmost source, in Burundi. A small pyramid there now marks Dr. Waldecker's discovery with the words "Caput Nili—Source of the Nile."

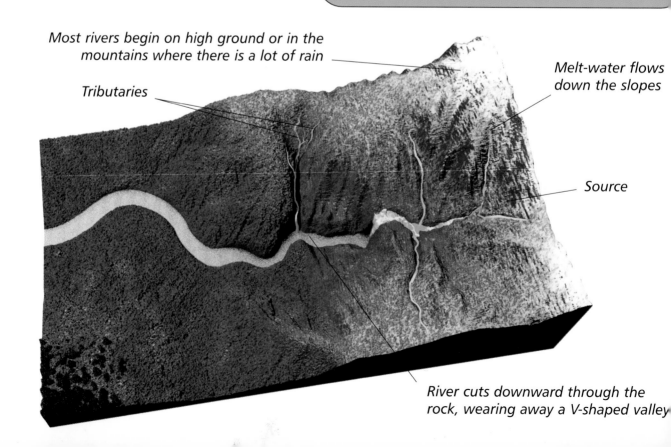

Most rivers begin on high ground or in the mountains where there is a lot of rain

Tributaries

Melt-water flows down the slopes

Source

River cuts downward through the rock, wearing away a V-shaped valley

Other rivers start from a source bubbling out of the rocks, called a spring. Some kinds of rock are **porous**—that is, water can sink into the rock. In areas of porous rock, such as sandstone or limestone, rainwater trickles through the rock and then flows underground until it emerges from the earth, forming a spring.

On low-lying ground and in depressions, water may gather in hollows, or on the surface of the land, causing the ground to be **saturated**. This is known as a bog, marsh, or swamp. Water trickles out of bogs into streams and rivers.

LOCATION FILE

THE RHINE AND RHÔNE

Two of Europe's great rivers, the Rhine (above) and the Rhône, flow from sources close together high in the Swiss Alps, but they flow out in opposite directions. The Rhine flows 862 miles (1,390 km) north and west, out through the Netherlands, and into the North Sea. It is an important shipping route. The 504-mile-long (813 km) Rhône flows south through France and out into the Mediterranean Sea. Its route passes through mountains, making it difficult for large ships to navigate.

Above: **Barges on the Rhine River. Since Roman times, the Rhine has been vitally important for travel and trade.**

DOWN THE MOUNTAIN

As rivers flow they loosen rocks and soil, especially when they flood. They may carry along great boulders and huge quantities of mud, transporting them to another place along the river's bed or sometimes carrying them all the way to the sea. The rocks are smashed and crushed into smaller pieces, then ground into tiny grains of sand called sediment. Soil is washed into the river by rainfall and adds to the river's sediment. Each of a river's tributaries brings sediment from the land it drains.

SEDIMENT

As long as the river is flowing quickly, sediment is carried along in the water. Where the water starts to flow more slowly, the sediment may fall to the bottom of the river's bed. This clogs up the river and makes it dangerous for larger boats traveling along its course. The sediment needs to be dug or **dredged** out of the river's bed to make it safe for boats again.

Some sediment is carried all the way to the river's mouth and into the sea. In Asia, the Ganges, Yellow River, and Brahmaputra carry one-fifth of the world's sediment into the sea.

The tributaries of the Amazon River are each a different color, because they bring sediment made up from the different kinds of soil and rock they flow over.

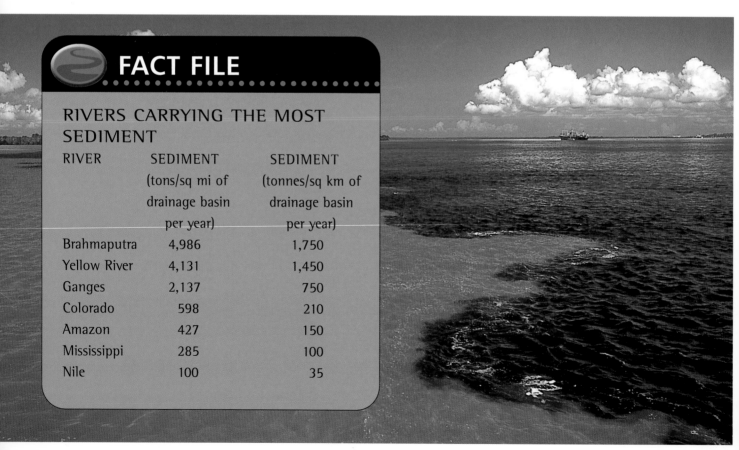

FACT FILE

RIVERS CARRYING THE MOST SEDIMENT

RIVER	SEDIMENT (tons/sq mi of drainage basin per year)	SEDIMENT (tonnes/sq km of drainage basin per year)
Brahmaputra	4,986	1,750
Yellow River	4,131	1,450
Ganges	2,137	750
Colorado	598	210
Amazon	427	150
Mississippi	285	100
Nile	100	35

FORESTS—OR FLOODS?

Tree roots help to hold the land together so that less soil is **eroded**, or carried away, as water runs across it. Trees and plants absorb rainwater in the soil, which also helps to prevent flooding. Where forests have been cut down, especially on steep hillsides, soil is more easily eroded, and this can lead to serious flooding and dangerous landslides.

Above: Deforestation in South Africa. Forests may be cut down, especially in poorer countries, for timber and to clear land for farming or construction.

LOCATION FILE

NORTHERN THAILAND

In December 2001, in the Phetchabun region of northern Thailand, more than 70 people were killed in **flash floods**. Relief work was hampered by mud and tree trunks that were swept down the mountainsides. Flash floods were always a problem in the region, but they have become more frequent and much more dangerous since huge areas of local forest were cut down.

Villagers search through a house badly damaged by a flash flood in the Phetchabun province of Thailand.

R iver valleys are formed in a constant process. As a river flows down over mountains and hills, it cuts down into the rock. Over hundreds of thousands of years, the flowing water can cut deep valleys and dramatic waterfalls, changing the landscape.

VALLEYS

Stones and gravel grind the river's bed, gouging out a narrow, V-shaped channel. In areas of softer rock, such as sandstone, rivers can erode the rock more quickly and dramatically than in areas of hard rock, such as granite.

During the ice age, glaciers cut great valleys as they flowed out toward the sea. Unlike rivers, glaciers form a wide, U-shaped valley. Active glaciers are still at work in cold regions around the world. The longest glacier in the world is in the Antarctic. It is 338 miles (515 km) long.

Some river valleys, called **wadis**, run through deserts. They are usually dry because so little rain falls in the desert. Wadis were formed thousands of years ago when Earth's climate was different from how it is today. Wadis were cut when there was enough rain to let rivers flow, but today wadis are filled only if exceptional rainfall causes a flash flood.

The action of a river carves a V-shaped valley.

The action of a glacier carves a U-shaped valley.

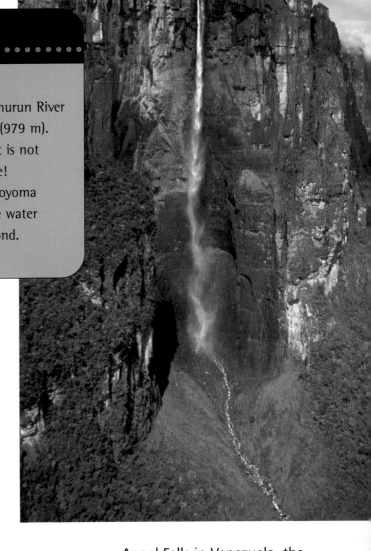

WATERFALLS

• The world's highest waterfall—Angel Falls (right), on the Churun River in Venezuela, South America—has a total drop of 3,211 feet (979 m).

• The widest waterfall is the Khon Cataracts, in Laos, Asia. It is not very deep, but measures more than seven miles (12 km) wide!

• The waterfall with the most water flowing per second is Boyoma Falls, in the Democratic Republic of Congo, Africa. There the water flows at a rate of 600,440 cubic feet (17,000 cu m) per second.

WATERFALLS AND RAPIDS

A waterfall is a place where a river drops vertically to a lower level. Many waterfalls are formed when a river flows over different kinds of rock. The water wears away soft rock more quickly than hard rock, so the hard rock remains while, over hundreds of thousands of years, the soft rock is eroded. This creates a cliff edge over which the water flows. Some spectacular waterfalls, called hanging valleys, are created by glaciers.

Rapids are places where the river drops quickly, but not as steeply as at a waterfall. Rapids form where the rock is too hard for the river to wear down evenly.

Angel Falls in Venezuela, the world's highest falls.

BLONDIN

In 1859, the French acrobat Jean-Francois Gravelet (1824-97), known as Blondin, crossed the Niagara gorge, just by the Falls, by tightrope between the U.S. and Canada. The tightrope was 1,099 feet (335 m) long, suspended 161 feet (49 m) above the water. He repeated the feat many times, backwards, blindfolded, and once sitting down midway to cook and eat an omelette!

Blondin, the French acrobat, performs a tightrope walk high above the Niagara River.

GORGES, CANYONS, CAVES

Gorges and canyons are very steep valleys, or gashes, in the landscape where a river has cut deep into the rock. Many caves are formed by rivers, too, where the water is flowing underground. Gorges, canyons, and caves all show the natural power of a river, eroding rock over millions of years.

Canyons can range in size from narrow slits in hard rock to enormous trenches. A river flows at the bottom, constantly carving away at the rock beneath.

The Grand Canyon, in the U.S., is the world's deepest, longest, and widest canyon. It was carved out by the Colorado River. Down its sides, the Grand Canyon reveals layers of different colored rock. These layers show the history of Earth's rocks. The oldest rocks are at the bottom. Some are up to four billion years old—among the oldest rocks on Earth.

FACT FILE

DEEP DOWN
• The Grand Canyon is 275 miles (443 km) long, and its steep walls are up to 5,697 feet (1,737 m) deep. At its widest point, the canyon measures 18 miles (29 km) wide.
• The deepest river in the world is China's Yangtze River. As it passes through the 1,968-foot-high (600 m) Three Gorges, the river flows up to 590 feet (180 m) deep. A new **dam** on the Yangtze River means that the rising water will eventually cover these gorges.

The rocks at the bottom of the Grand Canyon date from about two billion years ago, while those in the top layer are about 250 million years old. Rocks younger than 250 million years have eroded.

CAVES AND POTHOLES

Caves and potholes are created by underground rivers wearing away at the rock. Most caves are in areas where there are thick layers of limestone rock. Limestone is porous rock, so water can seep through it. The water flows underground along cracks between layers of rock. As more and more water flows through the cracks, they grow wider. The flowing water forms an underground river that is able to erode a cave out of the limestone. Underground rivers usually come to the surface through a spring or cave entrance.

Exploring caves, or potholing, is a popular hobby. Potholers squeeze through narrow cracks to try to find new caves. They use underwater equipment to swim along underground rivers. Potholing can be dangerous, especially if there is sudden heavy rain, which makes the underground river level rise.

An underground river wore away this large passage, called Clearwater Cave, in Mulu National Park, Sarawak, Malaysia. The cave is 66 miles (107 km) long.

 LOCATION FILE

WORLD'S LONGEST CAVE

The Mammoth Cave National Park and Flint Ridge Cave System, in Kentucky, together make up a 310-mile-long (500 km) network of underground caves, rivers, and lakes. More than 50 types of cave creatures have been discovered there, including blind fish and colorless spiders, specially adapted to life in this dark, watery environment.

MEANDERS AND LAKES

In the mountains, river water travels fast down steep slopes, but once a river reaches lower land, it flows more slowly. The river cuts a course through the softest bits of ground on its way to the sea, flowing in loops and curves, and carving out a wide valley bottom. Lakes may be formed where a river flows into a lower area of land.

MEANDERS

The loops and curves of a slow-moving river are called **meanders**. The water flows fastest around the outer edge of the meander, and over time this erodes the outer edge, gradually widening the valley. On the inner bank of each meander the water flows more slowly, depositing sediment there. This causes the entire meander system to advance slowly downstream.

Sometimes, when the river is in high flow or flood, it cuts across the neck of a meander to create a straighter path. This can leave a crescent-shaped lake called an oxbow lake. Oxbow lakes do not last very long, because they are no longer being filled by the river's flow. Over time they fill up with sediment and plants grow, forming bogs and swamps.

FACT FILE

WORLD'S LARGEST LAKES, 2001

LAKE	LOCATION	AREA
Caspian Sea	Asia	150,696 sq
		(386,400 sq
Lake Superior	North America	32,019 sq
		(82,100 sq
Lake Victoria	Africa	27,099 sq
		(69,485 sq
Lake Huron	North America	23,244 sq
		(59,600 sq
Lake Michigan	North America	22,542 sq
		(57,800 sq

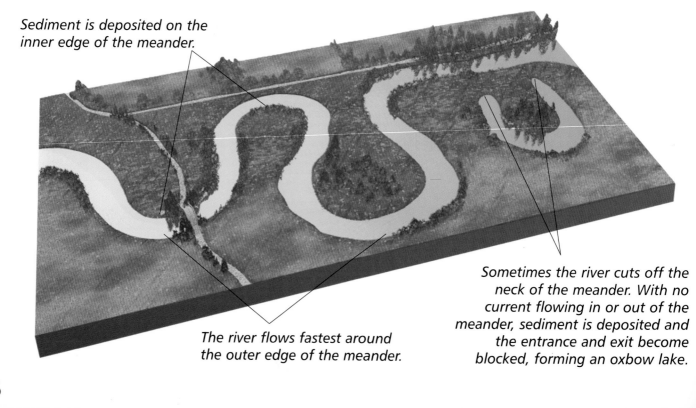

Sediment is deposited on the inner edge of the meander.

The river flows fastest around the outer edge of the meander.

Sometimes the river cuts off the neck of the meander. With no current flowing in or out of the meander, sediment is deposited and the entrance and exit become blocked, forming an oxbow lake.

16

The amazing contortions of a meandering river in Alaska. An oxbow lake can be seen in the center of the picture.

LAKES

Lakes are formed where a river flows through a hollow in the ground, or where the river is blocked. Water gathers and fills up the hollow. A stream or river flows out of the lowest edge of the lake. Some lakes, however, have no outflow, and lose water only by evaporation. In some cases, such as Australia's Lake Eyre, these lakes can become very salty as the minerals in the water become more concentrated. Some lakes are so large that they are called seas, even though they are enclosed by land.

 # LOCATION FILE ....

SHREWSBURY

The historic town of Shrewsbury (right), in the border country between England and Wales, is built on land contained within a loop of the Severn River. The river forms a natural defense around the walled town, which made it a safe stronghold during times of war in the Middle Ages.

This aerial view of Shrewsbury shows how the old town was built inside a loop of the river.

THE RIVER'S MOUTH

A river ends where it pours out its water into another river, into the sea, or, in some places, into a lake. This place is called the river's mouth. Here the river deposits its water, as well as all the mud and pollution it may have collected on the way.

Almost all river water flows out into the sea or the ocean, with a few exceptions. The Volga River, in Russia, for example, actually flows inland into the world's largest lake, the Caspian Sea. Many rivers flow into the sea with such force that they continue to flow for several miles after reaching the sea. The Amazon pours four times more water into the sea than the next biggest river, the Congo, in Africa. Water from the Amazon flows out into the salty sea water for 99 miles (160 km). The river water floats above the sea water, because freshwater is less dense than saltwater.

A view of the Yangtze River **delta** from space shows how the river empties into the sea.

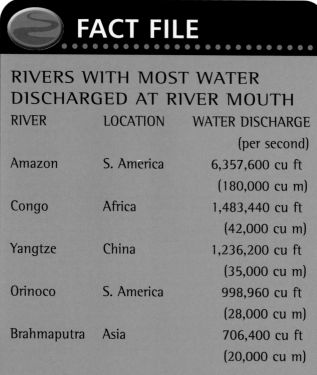

FACT FILE

RIVERS WITH MOST WATER DISCHARGED AT RIVER MOUTH

RIVER	LOCATION	WATER DISCHARGE (per second)
Amazon	S. America	6,357,600 cu ft (180,000 cu m)
Congo	Africa	1,483,440 cu ft (42,000 cu m)
Yangtze	China	1,236,200 cu ft (35,000 cu m)
Orinoco	S. America	998,960 cu ft (28,000 cu m)
Brahmaputra	Asia	706,400 cu ft (20,000 cu m)

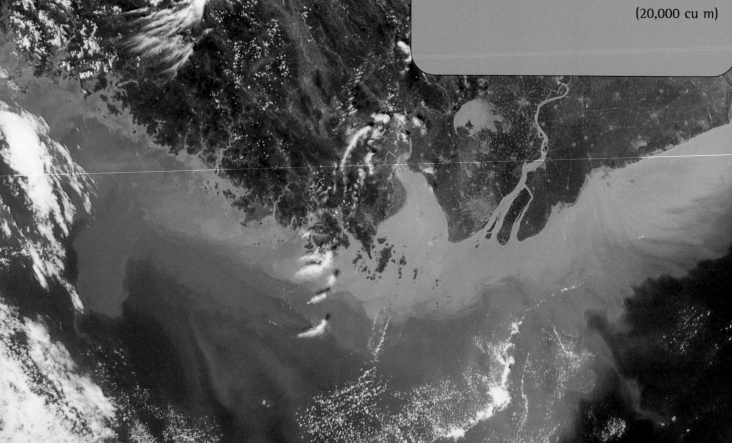

LOCATION FILE

THE WASH

In Norfolk, on the east coast of England, the river Ouse opens into a great estuary called the Wash (above). It is one of Europe's richest wildlife habitats. River meadows flood every winter for 19 miles (30 km) along the river's banks. There are also mudflats, salt marshes, and flooded gravel pits. Huge flocks of ducks, geese, and other birds migrate here from the Arctic north to spend the winter. In the summer, wading birds such as lapwings breed in the estuary.

Above: **Flocks of birds on a river estuary in Norfolk, UK.**

ESTUARIES

Most rivers grow wider as they flow into the sea. This wider area at the river's mouth is called an **estuary**. Here the river water meets the tidal water from the sea. When the tide is coming in, sea water flows back up into the estuary for some distance.

As the river opens out into the estuary, the water flows more slowly. The mud and sediment in its water drops to the bottom of the river's bed and along its banks. When the tide goes out, this river mud is left uncovered. These areas are called **mudflats**. At low tide, mudflats are an important wildlife habitat, offering rich feeding grounds for wading birds such as sandpipers, who dig with their beaks for burrowing creatures beneath the surface of the mud.

DELTAS AND SWAMPS

Deltas—the wide open mouths of many rivers—are so-called because they form a delta shape. Delta, or Δ, is the fourth letter in the Greek alphabet, equivalent to our "D." Its shape is how the Nile Delta looked to the ancient Greeks living to the north. The word "delta" is now used to describe a place where a river flows in many separate channels out into the sea. The Ganges, Amazon, Mississippi, and the Nile all form a delta where they meet the sea.

DELTA SHAPES

Deltas can form different shapes. Some deltas form the shape of an arc; others look like the outstretched fingers of a hand, or like a bird's foot. These deltas are called bird's foot deltas. Some deltas are very wide indeed, stretching for tens or even hundreds of miles.

Deltas are formed where a river slows down as it reaches the sea. Because it is flowing more slowly, the sediment and mud it has been carrying drops onto the river's bed and banks. As the delta builds up, the river creates small streams through which the water flows to the sea. These are called distributaries.

FACT FILE

DELTA SIZES
• The biggest delta in the world is formed by two great rivers, the Ganges and the Brahmaputra, in Bangladesh. Their joint delta covers an area of about 23,400 square miles (60,000 sq km).
• Swamps on the Mississippi Delta are shrinking by up to 39 square miles (100 sq km) a year, partly because dams are reducing the amount of sediment carried by the river, and because of reduced soil erosion from farming.

Salt marshes and low islands in the great Mississippi Delta.

LOW-LYING ISLANDS

Over many hundreds and thousands of years, layers of sediment build up. Grasses, reeds, and other marshy plants that can live in salty tide-water start to take root in the mud banks. Their roots stop the mud from being washed away. Very gradually, as the vegetation dies back and grows again, the mud changes into soil, and low, flat islands are formed in the river.

Low-lying land formed in a delta is often flooded when the river-level is high, or when storms and cyclones send huge waves crashing in from the sea. However, delta land is very fertile and it attracts people to live and farm there, even though there is great danger from flooding. In 1990, 140,000 people were killed by floods caused by a cyclone in the Ganges Delta.

LOCATION FILE

THE SUNDARBANS

In the Ganges River Delta, on the Bay of Bengal, there are more than 50 low islands, called the Sundarbans. The Sundarbans contains the largest area of mangrove trees in the world. Mangrove trees are like trees growing on stilts. Many rare creatures live in this unique habitat, including Bengal tigers, crocodiles, and golden eagles.

Above: **A fishing village in the Sundarbans, West Bengal, India.**

Right: **Rare Bengal tigers live in the mangrove swamps in the Sundarbans.**

RIVER WILDLIFE

A river is a rich and complex wildlife habitat. Rivers and river banks are the natural home for many kinds of fish, birds, insects, and other animals. Fish feed on smaller creatures as well as weeds, reeds, and algae. In turn, the fish provide a nourishing food source for birds, reptiles, and mammals—including humans.

VARIETY OF LIFE

Tropical rivers support an astounding range of wildlife. As well as fish, the Plata River, in South America, has caimans (a type of crocodile), many types of water snakes, frogs, toads, and freshwater crabs. Large birds such as herons, cormorants, and storks come to catch fish. Even in the coldest environments, rivers provide a habitat for a wide range of wildlife. The icy Ob River, in Siberia, for instance, has more than 50 species of fish.

In Africa, land animals come to the river bank to drink. Elephants need to drink 35 to 60 gallons (135–225 l) of water per day. Animals coming to drink may also feed on plants growing there, catch fish from the river, and prey on other animals that come to drink there.

Rivers provide vital drinking water for many animals, such as these lions.

BEAVERS

Beavers are large rodents. They live beside rivers and lakes, mostly in North America. Beavers build dams to make small lakes, where they are safe from predators. They build dams with twigs, branches, and logs, with layers of gravel or mud. Beaver dams can divert or block the flow of rivers and streams.

A beaver gnawing at a tree.

FOOD CHAINS

In the wild, animals survive by eating either plants or other animals. Living things are linked as if in a chain, each one being the food for the next one in the series. Plants are always at the bottom of the chain, with large, hunting animals at the top. For instance, pondweed is eaten by ducks, which are eaten by foxes. This pattern is called a food chain.

If one part of the food chain is harmed, other creatures in the chain will also be affected. If fish are poisoned by pollution, animals that eat the fish may be poisoned, too. If all the fish die, other animals may die because they have no food.

FACT FILE

SALMON MIGRATION

• Salmon breed in rivers. The young salmon then swim out to sea, but return as adults to breed, often traveling thousands of miles to swim back up the very river where they hatched.

• Salmon can identify a particular river by its smell.

• Some types of salmon die soon after breeding. Others survive to make the journey again.

A grizzly bear catches a salmon as it leaps up a waterfall.

HARVESTING THE RIVER

Since ancient times, humans have harvested rivers for fish and for plants, such as reeds. Ice was harvested from rivers, too, before the invention of refrigerators. Today, large-scale commercial production of fish is increasing.

All around the world, people living beside rivers **exploit** their produce. Fish, shellfish, and waterfowl provide a rich source of protein. On the Yenisey River, in Siberia, local people catch fish such as carp and perch, as well as sturgeon, whose eggs are prized as the luxury food caviar.

Food crops such as watercress and samphire provide vitamins and minerals. River plants such as reeds can be used for weaving or building roofs. Just as on land, river farmers encourage and develop crops that grow naturally in the river environment.

FISH FARMING

Wild fish stocks in the rivers and oceans are under threat as the fishing industry grows larger and more efficient. In many parts of the world, over-fishing has caused a huge drop in the number of fish. There are not enough fish left in the wild to breed and replace those that are caught. In response, fish farming is on the increase around the world.

Fishermen set their nets at the Yenisey River, in Siberia, Russia. The Yenisey has abundant fish of more than 30 different species.

Fish farms breed and grow fish to sell for food. This provides a steady supply of fish, without reducing the number of wild fish even further. Reduced fishing in the wild allows fish populations time to grow again.

There are fish farms in seas, lakes, **reservoirs**, and rivers; some are huge, commercial concerns, others are small, family businesses. Many types of fish and shellfish are grown and harvested in river fish farms. There are even alligator farms in rivers in hot and tropical areas.

PROTECTING RIVERS

Rivers are vital for the wildlife in the water and on the banks, and they are also important for humans, but they are fragile environments. Rivers are natural drains, which can become polluted when they are used to drain away chemical or industrial waste. Building on or near riverbanks reduces the habitat available for wildlife.

Most people's drinking water comes from rivers and reservoirs. In developed countries, water is purified, or cleaned, before it is delivered to people's homes. Unfortunately, in many of the world's poorest countries people have no choice but to use rivers for drinking, washing, and sometimes for carrying away untreated sewage. Millions of people around the world have no clean drinking water. Drinking dirty water can bring poor health and dangerous diseases.

A woman in Nepal has to wash her pots in a polluted river.

FACT FILE

POLLUTION ACCIDENTS
• In January 2000, huge amounts of cyanide-laden water spilled out of an abandoned mine in Romania into the rivers Szamos and Tisza. All living creatures were killed in a 248-mile (400 km) stretch of the river. Fortunately, the rivers have now recovered.
• Thousands of fish and birds were killed in the Guadiamar River, in Spain, in 1998, when poisonous sludge spilled into a river after a mine reservoir broke its banks.

THE GRANDMOTHER OF THE GLADES

Marjory Stoneman Douglas (1890-1998) was an early U.S. environmental campaigner. In 1947, her book River of Grass began a public campaign to protect mangrove swamps at the Mississippi Delta, an important wildlife habitat. In 1993, at the age of 103, she was awarded a Presidential Medal for her work defending the Mississippi River's ecosystem.

Above: **Marjory Stoneman Douglas examines a grass stalk in the Florida Everglades.**

POLLUTION

Rivers and streams can become polluted in many ways, such as when waste from factories is poured into them, or when pesticides used in farming run off the soil and into streams and rivers, harming the wildlife in and around them. Another threat is from old coal, lead, and tin mines. When old mines are closed, the mining tunnels and shafts fill up with water, and the water becomes polluted by the metal and rusty machinery. The dirty water flows away, eventually joining a stream or river.

CAMPAIGNING TO PROTECT THE ENVIRONMENT

Many countries have passed laws to try to keep rivers clean and to protect the environment. Farmers and companies who pollute rivers with chemicals, or by dumping waste, must pay large fines. Environmental groups campaign for stronger protection for rivers and wildlife, and to provide clean drinking water for everyone on the planet. As a result of this, river water is improving now throughout the industrialized world, after centuries of increasing pollution.

RIVER CIVILIZATIONS

The earliest human civilizations were built near rivers in Egypt, India, and China. Rivers provided a natural water supply, and people could travel and transport goods down a river more easily than across land before roads were built.

FIRST CITIES

The world's first cities grew up around 5,000 years ago in Mesopotamia (modern Turkey, Iraq, and Syria). The name "Mesopotamia," in Greek, means "the land between two rivers." These two rivers, the Tigris and the Euphrates, flooded their banks every spring. The regular flooding laid down a rich layer of fertilizing mud that made the surrounding plains rich and fertile for planting crops. The human population flourished with plentiful food supplies, and cities developed.

The civilization of ancient Egypt also depended on the flooding of a river, the Nile. The Nile valley is a long, narrow, fertile strip of land surrounded by hot, dry desert. Boats linked the north and south of the country, traveling along the Nile downstream on the current, and upstream using sails.

EARLY FARMING

The farmers of Mesopotamia and ancient Egypt built complex **irrigation** systems to bring water to their crops. **Canals**, ditches, and reservoirs controlled and channeled the annual floods. Irrigation allowed crops to be grown, including wheat, vegetables, and fruit. Flax (a type of plant) was woven to make linen for clothing, sails, and ropes. In Egypt, papyrus was grown to produce a type of paper. Thus rivers enabled early human technologies and the development of agriculture.

A worker with a modern irrigation pump bringing water from the Nile River to farmland in Egypt. River water is still vital for agriculture, just as it was in ancient times.

The Ganges River, holy to Hindus, is the scene for many cremations.

SYMBOLISM

Rivers are so important to human life that they feature in many religions around the world. They often symbolize a barrier that divides life from death. Sometimes their flow represents the eternal flow of life.

FACT FILE

RIVERS' RELIGIOUS SYMBOLISM

- In Hinduism, the main religion of India, the Ganges River is a holy river. Funerals take place along its banks.
- In Christianity, St. Christopher carried Jesus Christ as a child across a river.
- In Greek mythology, the souls of the dead had to be ferried over the river Styx on their journey to the Underworld.

Below: **The Indus River flows from its source in Tibet to the Arabian Sea.**

LOCATION FILE

INDUS VALLEY

The Indus River (right) flows through the Punjab, in modern Pakistan. More than 4,500 years ago, villages and towns grew up along 1,240 miles (2,000 km) of the Indus Valley. Farmers grew a wide range of food crops and the earliest types of cotton. Domesticated animals were raised including dogs, cattle, and even elephants! Gold and silver were traded from as far away as India and Afghanistan.

RIVERS AND TECHNOLOGY

Rivers have been used since ancient times for transportation and as a source of power. Over the centuries, developing technology has found ways to improve rivers for transportation, and harness them as a source of power for industry.

CANALIZING RIVERS

A river that boats can travel along is said to be navigable. Many rivers have been changed to make them more navigable for large cargo ships. For instance, the Rhine River, in Germany, has been dredged to make it deeper and it is now navigable for more than 496 miles (800 km). Meanders on the Mississippi River have been straightened to let larger boats pass. After these changes, a river is said to be canalized, that is, more like a canal, although the water is still flowing.

Boats cannot travel where a river drops too steeply, but one answer is to build a lock and **weir**. A weir is a small step built across the river, and a lock is a small, enclosed section of the river in which the water level can be raised or lowered to allow boats to reach the water level above or below the weir.

The vastness of the Mississippi River is seen here, where dozens of barges are herded together and transported downriver.

FACT FILE

CHINA'S WATERWAYS

• In 1949, China's new Communist government set about building a national network of waterways. Now China has more than 62,000 miles (100,000 km) of navigable waterways.

• The Grand Canal, running 1,091 miles (1,760 km) from Beijing to Hangzhou, is the longest canal in the world. It was begun more than 2,400 years ago.

• On the mountainous Yangtze and Wu Rivers, cables pull boats safely over dangerous rapids.

BENOIT FOURNEYRON

In 1827, a young Frenchman named Benoit Fourneyron invented the water **turbine**, a much smaller and more efficient version of the traditional huge waterwheel. During Fourneyron's lifetime, scientists scoffed at his invention, but his work was far ahead of its time. In 1895, 30 years after Fourneyron died, turbines were installed at Niagara Falls to turn generators to produce electricity. Turbines are still widely in use today.

WATER POWER

River power has been in use since Roman times, when mills built beside rivers had large wooden waterwheels that turned a grindstone to grind grain or perform other tasks. In the 19th century, during the Industrial Revolution, factories sprang up wherever there was enough water to turn waterwheels. Waterwheels powered factory machinery, such as looms. In the 20th century, new technology has been developed to harness water power to create electricity. This is called **hydroelectricity** (see pages 34 and 35).

This waterwheel was built in the 19th century to power a sawmill in Sherbrooke, Nova Scotia, Canada. Sherbrooke village is now a living history museum.

CROSSING THE RIVER

A river forms a natural barrier. Crossing the river safely—above, through, or even under the water—is a great challenge to human ingenuity. Through the ages, new technology, materials, and designs have developed to solve the ancient problem of crossing rivers.

The simplest way of crossing a stream or small river is to wade through at a shallow point, called a ford. Villages grew up at these traditional crossing points. Place names such as Bedford or Stratford often reflect their origin.

Around the world, the first bridges were built out of natural materials, including stone blocks, felled tree trunks, or ropes woven out of reeds or vines. The Romans were the first to develop arched bridges. The first metal bridge was built of iron in 1779, over the Severn River at Ironbridge in the UK.

Over the past 200 years, revolutionary bridge designs have developed as new materials have come into use, including steel and reinforced concrete—concrete reinforced with metal inside. Today, most bridges are built out of concrete.

FACT FILE

BRIDGE FACTS
• The Runyang Bridge, across the mouth of the Yangtze River, in China, is due for completion in 200 It will be the longest river crossing in the world. Its longest span is 4,887 feet (1,490 m), and its total length is 14 miles (23 km).
• The Gateshead Millennium Bridge, over the Tyne River, in northeastern England, opened in 2001. It is known as the "blinking eye" bridge because it tips up—looking like a blinking eyelid—to let ships pass underneath.
• There are no bridges at all across the Amazon Rive It is too wide to bridge safely. When the Amazon floods, it can measure 30 miles (48 km) wide!

The Gateshead Millennium Bridge is seen here tipped up to allow ships to pass under it. The bridge provides a footpath and bike path linking the cities of Gateshead and Newcastle upon Tyn

The Jiangyin Bridge, over the Yangtze River, in China, is a suspension bridge with a longest span of 4,543 feet (1,385 m), making it the world's second-longest cable-suspended river bridge, after the Humber Bridge, in the UK.

TUNNELS AND FERRIES

Tunneling under a river is another way to cross the water. The first tunnel under the Thames River, in London, was completed in 1843. In 1998, work began on two double-decker road tunnels totaling 11 miles (18 km) under the river Seine, in Paris, France, preserving the beauty of the river valley.

Ferries are another way of crossing a river, and they range from simple rowing boats to double- or triple-decker ships carrying cars, trucks, and cargo.

Some ferries are very simple, like this boat in Bangladesh, crossing the Meghna River.

DAMS AND RESERVOIRS

Rivers provide drinking water, but because rivers' flow can change, they are unreliable sources of water. Building a dam is a way of allowing valuable freshwater to be stored and used when it is needed. Over the last 100 years, dams have been developed to provide a renewable source of energy as well.

A dam is a wall across a river which stops the water from flowing onward. Small dams can be built out of earth and rocks, but modern, giant dams are built out of concrete. The 984-foot-high (300 m) Nurek Dam, on the Vakhsh River, in Tajikistan, is the highest in the world.

When a dam is built, the water rises behind it to fill the river valley. It forms an artificial lake, called a reservoir. Water is then let out in a regular flow, through drains in the dam. This is safer and more reliable than the river's seasonal changes.

This diagram shows how a dam works.

LOCATION FILE

THREE GORGES DAM ON CHINA'S YANGTZE RIVER

The Three Gorges Dam will be the largest hydroelectric dam in the world—more than .6 miles (1 km) across, with a reservoir stretching more than 347 miles (560 km) upstream. In 1989, local people's protests forced the Chinese government to suspend its plans for the dam, but construction work finally began in 1994, and the dam is now nearing completion.

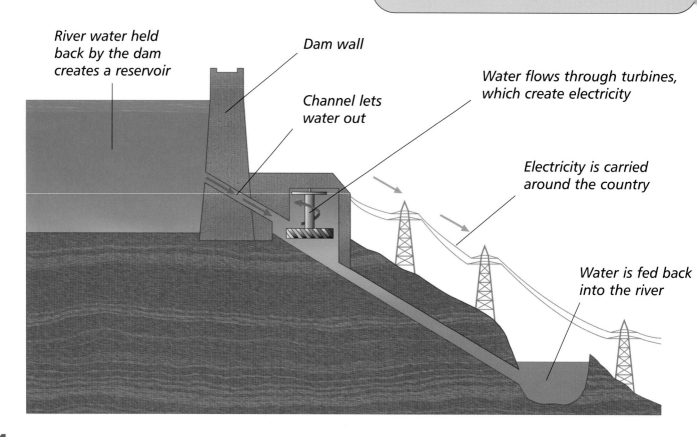

River water held back by the dam creates a reservoir

Dam wall

Channel lets water out

Water flows through turbines, which create electricity

Electricity is carried around the country

Water is fed back into the river

HYDROELECTRICITY

The power of water flowing out through a dam can be harnessed to create hydroelectricity. As the water flows it turns turbines in the dam's drains, which generate electricity. The Hoover Dam, on the Colorado River, was completed in 1936. It was one of the earliest hydroelectric dams. Its reservoir, Lake Mead, is one of the largest artificial lakes in the world.

Hydroelectric dams can be productive, but they are hugely expensive to construct. The electricity may be too costly for ordinary local people. The environmental impact on the area is enormous, as the rising water drowns villages and towns in the valley. Hundreds of thousands of people can lose their homes when a large dam is built. Protestors argue that these huge projects are too expensive in poor, developing countries—especially if many people will lose their homes as a result.

The Glen Canyon Dam, in Utah, which was completed in 1963. It altered the flow of the Colorado River and has changed the ecosystem.

 FACT FILE

DAM DISASTERS

• Almost 5,000 years ago, a dam on the Nile River failed during its first flood season. It was not correctly designed.

• A flash flood in 1889 in Pennsylvania caused a dam to break. Two thousand people were killed in an hour.

• In 1963, a landslide fell into the Vaiont Dam reservoir in Italy, producing a huge wave of water over the dam and killing 3,000 people. The dam was not seriously damaged.

ESTUARY ENERGY

Some river estuaries offer a source of renewable energy: tidal energy. In the estuary, the river water mixes with the sea, flowing back and forth with the tides. The tide level rises and falls twice a day, and this tidal change can be harnessed to generate electricity.

TIDE MILLS

Tidal energy has been used for centuries. From the 11th century onward, tide mills were built on river estuaries in the UK and along the Atlantic coasts of France and Spain. Most mills were used for grinding grain, and at Woodbridge, on the Deben River, in East Anglia, UK, the ancient tide mill is still working today. Centuries later, tide mills were built on river estuaries along the Atlantic coast in the U.S. and in Guyana, South America. They were used to crush sugar cane to produce sugar.

A traditional tidal mill on the river Rance, in France, at low tide.

FACT FILE

RENEWABLE ENERGY
• In 2001, renewable energy made up only six percent of America's energy consumption.
• Renewable energy such as tidal energy is up to four times more costly than traditional fossil fuels such as coal or gas. But costs are falling as the technology develops.
• Governments around the world support the development of renewable energy. Wind energy is currently the fastest-developing source of renewable energy.

River estuaries such as this one in Nova Scotia, Canada, with a big difference between low and high tide, are the best sites for tidal power stations.

TIDAL ENERGY

In modern times, tidal power stations have been built or planned on river estuaries around the world. They are best placed where there is a big difference between high and low tide. At the Bay of Fundy, in Canada, the difference can be up to 66 feet (20 m), the greatest in the world. Here, rapids are caused on the St. John River by tidal water surging back up-river from the bay. Tidal energy was first considered in the Bay of Fundy in the 1920s, but it has always been found to be too expensive and damaging to area wildlife.

The Cardiff Bay Barrage, in Wales, has created a huge freshwater lake on the estuaries of the rivers Taff and Ely. Planners are exploring its potential for creating tidal energy. However, estuary mudflats offer important feeding and breeding grounds for many wading birds and other wildlife. Critics say that building estuary tidal power stations will harm a precious wildlife environment. So far, only a handful of tidal power stations have been constructed, the first being at La Rance, France (see box below for more information).

LOCATION FILE

LA RANCE ESTUARY POWER STATION

The tidal power station at La Rance, France, opened in 1966. Across the 2,460-foot-wide (750 m) estuary of the Rance River is a barrage, or barrier. Tidal water can flow through the barrage in either direction. As the water flows, it turns generators that make electricity. The power station produces energy for around one million households.

La Rance estuary power station.

RIVERS IN FLOOD

When a river floods, water rises up and washes over its banks. The water can spread very quickly over flat land on either side. Some river floods, such as on the Nile, are regular and usually safe. Other floods are great disasters, causing huge damage and loss of life.

Rivers can flood for a number of reasons. Most floods happen when there is very heavy rainfall or rapid melting of snow. If the ground is already very wet and cannot take in any more water, the rain runs quickly into rivers, which rise and cause flooding. Floods can also be caused by high tides sweeping upriver from the sea.

Flood disasters are one of the most costly natural disasters, sometimes killing hundreds or thousands of people. Rushing water brings torrents of mud and debris, and causes massive damage to homes, industry, and agriculture. Vital services such as roads, railways, and sewage systems can be swept away. When the Mississippi flooded in 1993, 30,000 homes were damaged. Repairs cost at least $10 billion. The Yellow River has earned the nickname "China's Sorrow," as it has caused some of the worst natural disasters of all time.

LOCATION FILE

THE RIVER ARNO, FLORENCE

The city of Florence, in northwest Italy, is famous for its historic art and architecture. In November 1966, the Arno River flooded to its highest level in 600 years. More than 1,000 paintings, 300,000 rare books, and 700,000 historic documents were soaked or covered in black, smelly slime. Repair work went on for many years afterwards.

People using a makeshift raft in a flooded street of Florence, during the flood of 1966.

HUMAN INFLUENCE

In many parts of the world, floods are growing more serious because of human influence. As well as cutting down forests, people are building more homes, roads, and paved areas, as the world's population grows. These buildings make it harder for water to be absorbed into the ground. In cities, networks of drains carry the water quickly into the rivers. As a result, cities send more water at greater speed into the rivers than is natural. Building is also taking place on natural floodplains, with a high risk of flooding. All these factors make flooding more likely to happen—and more dangerous when it does.

People in Mozambican floods in February 2000 wait on a rooftop to be rescued.

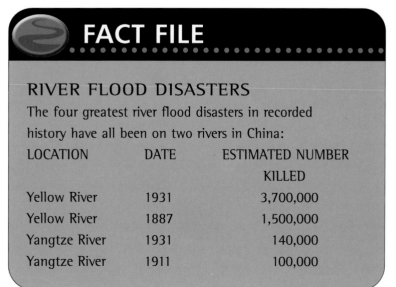

FACT FILE

RIVER FLOOD DISASTERS

The four greatest river flood disasters in recorded history have all been on two rivers in China:

LOCATION	DATE	ESTIMATED NUMBER KILLED
Yellow River	1931	3,700,000
Yellow River	1887	1,500,000
Yangtze River	1931	140,000
Yangtze River	1911	100,000

FLOOD DEFENSES

Floods are very dangerous, but building flood defenses helps to reduce the risk. Some types of flood defenses are very expensive, but there are many cheaper ways for people to live safely near rivers.

LEVEES

One defense from flooding is to build a wall on top of the natural banks of the river, called a levee (LEV-ay). Levees contain the river at a higher level without the water spilling over the top and flooding. Levees are built of concrete or, more cheaply, of earth and rock. At times of flood alert, the levee can be made higher still with sandbags, rocks, and soil. There is the danger, though, that the extra water is carried farther downstream to flood elsewhere.

Above: **Levees along the Garonne River, in France, protect Toulouse from the river breaking its banks and flooding the city.**

LOCATION FILE

THE THAMES BARRIER

The river Thames flows through London, and for years people worried about how to protect London from flooding caused by high tides and stormy winds. A large flood barrier (below) was completed in 1982. It has 10 separate gates that can be closed when there is danger of a flood. This high-tech type of flood defense is effective, but expensive to construct.

The Thames Barrier in London, UK.

DREDGING

Another method of reducing the risk of flooding is to clear, or dredge, riverbeds to remove sediment and rocks that have gathered there, clogging it up. Clearing allows the river to hold more water.

PLANTING

Another solution is to plant trees on land near rivers. Trees remove water from the ground and release it into the air, which reduces the amount of water running down hillsides into streams and rivers. The tree roots also help to bind the earth together, reducing soil erosion—which in turn reduces the amount of sediment clogging up rivers.

SAFER BUILDING

In some heavily populated areas where land is in short supply, homes are built on low-lying land, which is more at risk of flooding. Building homes on higher ground is a much safer policy.

Dredging a harbor in Germany. Dredging makes the riverbed deeper so that large ships can use the river.

FACT FILE

ANCIENT AND MODERN FLOOD DEFENSES

• In ancient Egypt, 595 miles (960 km) of levees were built along the west bank of the Nile River, from Aswan to the Mediterranean.

• Levees were first built on the banks of the Mississippi River in the early 18th century.

• More than 3,472 miles (5,600 km) of raised levees have been built along the Mississippi and its tributaries, but some are now being removed, as they are costly to maintain, and they simply shift the problem of flooding downstream. Instead, certain areas are set aside to take floodwater where it can do no harm.

LEISURE AND TOURISM

Rivers are great places to relax and have fun. Rivers attract anglers, walkers, and campers who enjoy the natural surroundings. New river sports such as whitewater rafting are growing in popularity. Leisure use of rivers is increasing as tourism grows around the world, but tourism brings its own dangers to wildlife and the environment.

FISHING

Angling, or fishing, is an ancient sport. A 2,400-year-old Chinese account tells of fishing with a silk line, using cooked rice as bait. In many countries today, more people take part in angling than in any other sport. As angling is restricted in many rivers to protect fish stocks, fishing in artificial lakes stocked with freshwater fish has become popular.

Some campaigners argue that fishing is a cruel sport that harms fish and other wildlife. Fishing lines, lead weights, and nets can harm birds and fish if they are left in the water. Anglers argue that they help to look after the environment and protect fish.

LOCATION FILE

RIVER SJOA, NORWAY
Norway's Sjoa River is a popular destination for whitewater rafting and many other outdoor sports. From a base at Randsverk, high in the mountains, vacationers can try out mountaineering, potholing (exploring caves), and fishing, as well as whitewater rafting.

An American whitewater rafting team battles with the waters of the Zambezi River, in Africa.

NEW RIVER SPORTS

Canoeing, or kayaking, became a popular sport in the 19th century. Canoeing became an Olympic event for the first time in 1924. In 1972, canoe slalom or whitewater canoeing was introduced as a new Olympic event, where canoes had to navigate through gates, rapids, and falls in a river. New river sports are developing all the time, including hydro glisse (from the French, meaning "water sliding"), which involves riding down a river holding onto a special board.

Travel companies offer whitewater rafting vacations in wild and beautiful surroundings, on rivers such as the Zambezi, in Africa. Tourism brings many benefits to local traders, but it can also threaten fragile ecosystems. Too many tourists visiting a region damage the very environment that attracted them in the first place.

Families enjoy a beach on the Rhine River, in Germany. The Rhine was extensively cleaned up in the 1970s and 1990s, having become badly polluted.

 FACT FILE

RIVER TOURISM AROUND THE WORLD

• Turkey's government is developing river sports tourism on the Göksu River, while protecting its important bird wildlife.

• In 2002, Cambodia, Laos, and Vietnam spent $35 million to attract tourists to the Mekong River, in Asia. Piers, walking trails, and information centers were built along the river.

• Botswana, in southern Africa, has developed a National Eco-Tourism Strategy for the Chobe River to develop tourism and conserve the environment.

RIVERS FOR LIFE

Fresh water from rivers is a vital resource for life. Modern daily life, especially in developed countries in the West, demands more and more fresh water for industry, agriculture, and homes. We must protect and share Earth's river water fairly to preserve life and the environment for the future.

USING WATER

In the West, each person uses 20 times more water than in the poorest countries. New methods of agriculture need extra irrigation; for example, growing luxury crops such as flowers in hot climates. This means more and more water is diverted from rivers, especially in countries where rainfall is very low and crops need more irrigation.

A bridge over the Yellow River, in China, where it ran dry in 1997.

The amount of water drawn from a river needs to be controlled and managed, because if too much water is taken out of a river it can dwindle or run dry. People living downstream may not have enough water, and the remaining water may become heavily polluted. Many rivers around the world are running dry. China's Yellow River ran dry in its lower reaches for seven months in 1997. This deprived Shadong Province of its water for irrigation. Shadong produces one-fifth of China's maize and one-seventh of its wheat.

FACT FILE

RIVERS IN TROUBLE

• The level of the inland Aral Sea in Asia has dropped by more than 52 feet (16 m) in the past 50 years. This is because so much water is taken out of its two main source rivers.
• More than 90 percent of the natural flow of the Nile River is used for irrigation or is lost through evaporation, especially from reservoirs.
• One in four people in the world does not have clean drinking water, and has no choice but to drink from polluted rivers or wells.

A child drinks from a tap bringing clean water, installed by the charity WaterAid. WaterAid is dedicated to providing safe water, sanitation, and hygiene education to the world's poorest people.

WATER IN WAR—AND PEACE

Water is such a precious resource for life that it can be a target during war. During many wars in the 20th century, dams have been bombed to destroy the water supply for industry and to cause flooding. In 1999, Serbian forces contaminated water supplies during the war in Kosovo.

Water wars may arise in the future where there are rival claims to water. To avoid this danger, many countries are working together to share and protect river water flowing through their lands. For instance, the Zambezi River crosses or forms the boundaries of six countries in southern Africa. International agreements between some of these countries have helped to share the water more fairly, to protect those downstream.

 ## LOCATION FILE

MEKONG RIVER, ASIA

Four of the countries along the Mekong River—Cambodia, Laos, Thailand, Vietnam—signed an agreement in 1995 to safeguard the river. They agreed to protect the water and the river environment, to protect shipping rights, and to make joint decisions about how much water to take out of the river.

GLOSSARY

Canals Narrow, man-made waterways, made for irrigation or for boats to travel along.

Canyons Deep gorges or ravines.

Condense Turn from a vapor into a liquid; for example, turn from steam into water.

Dam A wall built across a river or stream to hold back water.

Delta A place where a river flows in many channels out into the sea.

Discharge The amount of water flowing in a river.

Drainage area The area of land that drains into a river.

Dredged Scooped soil and sediment from the bottom of a river to deepen or clear it.

Eroded Wore away rocks and soil by water, wind, or ice.

Estuary The wide, tidal part of a river, where it leads into the sea.

Exploit To make use of, to make gain out of.

Flash floods Sudden, severe floods caused by heavy rain.

Glaciers Huge frozen rivers of slow-moving ice.

Groundwater Fresh water that is underground, contained within the rocks and soil.

Hydroelectricity Electricity that is generated when flowing water turns a turbine, usually in a dam.

Irrigation Supplying crop plants with water via channels or pipes in order to help them to grow.

Meanders Loops and curves made by a slow-moving river.

Mudflats The muddy area revealed at the mouth of a river when the tide is out.

Porous Having little holes that allow water to pass through.

Rapids A steep section of a river where the water flows fast over rocks.

Renewable energy Energy created from sources such as water, wind, and sun that are not used up by creating the energy.

Reservoirs Artificial lakes for storing water.

Saturated Holding as much water or liquid as it is able to.

Sediment Little bits of rocks and soil that are carried by a river.

Source The origin or head of a river.

Springs Sources or outflows of water from a rock.

Tributaries Streams that run into one another.

Turbine A rotary motor, with a wheel or drum with curved fins, that is driven by water or steam to generate electricity.

Wadis Beds of ancient rivers that ran through deserts.

Water cycle The circulation of Earth's water, in which it evaporates from the sea, lakes, and rivers to the air, and turns back to a liquid to fall as rain or snow.

Weir A dam across a river.

FURTHER INFORMATION

WEB SITES TO VISIT

http://www.irn.org

News about International Rivers Network's efforts to support local communities working to protect their rivers.
International Rivers Network
1847 Berkeley Way
Berkeley, CA 94703
Tel: (510) 848-1155
E-mail: info@irn.org

http://www.wateraid.org.uk

WaterAid is an international, non-governmental organization dedicated to providing safe water, sanitation, and hygiene education to the world's poorest people.
WaterAid
Prince Consort House, 27–29 Albert Embankment
London SE1 7UB, UK
Tel: +44 20 7793 4500
E-mail: wateraid@wateraid.org

http://www.wrc.wa.gov.au/protect/waterways/index.htm

The Web site of Waterways WA, Western Australia's waterways management program, about protecting rivers, creeks, wetlands, and estuaries.
Waterways and Rivers Commission
P.O. Box 6740, Hay Street
East Perth 6892, Western Australia
Tel: +61 08 9278 0300
E-mail: waterways.wa@wrc.wa.gov.au

BOOKS TO READ

Cumming, David. *Nile*. Milwaukee, Wisc.: Gareth Stevens, 2003.

Dramer, Kim. *Yellow River*. New York: Franklin Watts, 2001.

Lauber, Patricia. *Flood*. Washington, D.C.: National Geographic Society, 1996.

Morris, Neil. *Rivers*. Austin, Tex.: Raintree Steck-Vaughn, 1997.

INDEX